ART NOUVEAU DECORATIVE IRONWORK

137 Photographic Illustrations

Selected by
THEODORE MENTEN

Dover Publications, Inc.
New York

Frontispiece: Stair railing and elevator gate, 110 boulevard Raspail, Paris. Eugène Chifflot, architect.

Published in Canada by General Publishing Company, Ltd., 30 Lesmill Road, Don Mills, Toronto, Ontario.
Published in the United Kingdom by Constable and Company, Ltd.

Art Nouveau Decorative Ironwork, first published by Dover Publications, Inc., in 1981, is a selection of photographs from
  Ferronnerie de style moderne (first and second series). Paris, C. Schmid, no date.
  Ferronnerie moderne & de style modernisé (third series). Paris, C. Schmid & Ch. Massin, no date.

International Standard Book Number: 0-486-23986-1
Library of Congress Catalog Card Number: 81-65035

Manufactured in the United States of America
Dover Publications, Inc.
180 Varick Street
New York, N.Y. 10014

ALPHABETICAL LIST OF DESIGNERS, IRONWORKERS AND ARCHITECTS

ART NOUVEAU
DECORATIVE
IRONWORK

The captions supply virtually all the information contained in the original French editions. Where the designer/maker of the ironwork is known, his name is given as the first element in the caption. All buildings are located in Paris unless indicated otherwise.

1. Milinaire Frères. Entrance to an apartment building, 7, bis, rue Damrémont. Torchet & Gridaine, architects.

2. A. Dondelinger. Entrance to a large building, 103 rue Jouffroy.
Théodore Petit, architect.

3. A. Dondelinger. Entrance to an apartment house, 3 square Rapp.
J. Lavirotte, architect.

4. J. Salvanhac. Entrance, cast iron and chasing. E. Autant, architect.

5. J. Liet. Entrance to an apartment house, 155 rue de Grenelle.
J. Lavirotte, architect.

6. D'Hière. Wrought-iron grille for a room in a town house.

7. Gilt wrought-iron gate for a room in a town house, rue de Lota.

8. Wrought-iron stair railing in a town house, Brussels. Delpy, architect.

9. Wrought-iron and gilt stair case in a town house, Brussels. Victor Horta,
architect.

10. Wrought-iron and gilt stair railing in a town house, Brussels. Victor Horta, architect.

11. Stair railing in an apartment house, 50 avenue Victor-Hugo. Charles
Plumet, architect.

12. Wrought-iron and gilt stair railing in a town house, Brussels. Victor Horta, architect.

13. Wrought-iron stair railing, 17 rue Damrémont. H. Sauvage &
Ch. Sarazin, architects.

14. Entrance to an apartment house, 46 rue Spontini. L. Benouville,
architect.

15. Wrought-iron entrance to an apartment house, 22 rue Laugier.
H. Sauvage & Ch. Sarazin, architects.

16. Entrance to a large building, 5 rue Eugène-Labiche. Roth, architect.

17. Desjardins. Entrance to an apartment house, 4 rue Hermel.
L. P. Marquet, architect.

18. A. Dondelinger. Entrance to an apartment house, 134 rue de Grenelle.
J. Lavirotte, architect.

19. Entrance to a large building, 153 rue Lamarck. L. Dupont, architect.

20. Schwartz & Meurer. Entrance to an apartment house, 76 avenue d'Italie. G. Just & E. Denis, architects.

21. Verneuil. Entrance to an apartment house, 50 avenue de Ségur.
G. Ruprich-Robert, architect.

22. Entrance to a large building, 76 rue Nollet. L. Dupont, architect.

23. Entrance to a large building, place de l'Opéra. Roger Bouvard,
architect.

24. Peletan. Entrance to an apartment house, 40 boulevard Garibaldi.
A. M. Pellissier, architect.

25. A. Dondelinger. Entrance to an apartment house, 25 boulevard
Garibaldi. A. M. Pellissier, architect.

26. Schwartz & Meurer. Entrance to an apartment house, 30 avenue
Daumesnil. Designed by R. Chapuis; Emile Thomas, architect.

27. Entrance to an apartment house, 72 avenue d'Orléans. Eugène Petit,
architect.

28. A. Dondelinger. Entrance to a town house, 23 avenue de Messine.
J. Lavirotte, architect.

29. A. Dondelinger. Entrance to an apartment house, 6 rue de Messine.
J. Lavirotte, architect.

30. Entrance to a large building, 39 boulevard Raspail. Gustave Goy,
architect.

31. Bernard. Entrance to a large building, 53 rue Jouffroy.

32. A. Dondelinger. Wrought-iron stair railing, 9 rue Claude-Chahu.
Charles Klein, architect.

33. Alfred Bellard. Staircase in the town house of Prince Roland Bonaparte.
E. & A. Janty, architect.

34. A. Dondelinger. Entrance to an apartment house, 9 rue Claude-Chahu.
Charles Klein, architect.

35. Entrance to a town house, 520 avenue Louise, Brussels. Victor Horta, architect.

36. Delisle Frères. Wrought-iron gate to a room.

37. A. Dondelinger. Entrance to a town house. J. Lavirotte, architect.

38. Entrance to a large building, 1, bis, rue Félix-Ziem. P. Marteroy,
architect.

39. Entrance to an apartment house, 14, ter, rue Oudinot. Gustave Goy,
architect.

40. E. Robert. Wrought-iron entrance to a town house, 41 boulevard
Suchet. C. Ducharme, architect.

41. Entrance to a large building, 17 boulevard Flandrin. A. Pellechet,
architect.

42. Entrance to a town house, rue Américaine, Brussels. Victor Horta,
architect.

43. Entrance to a town house, rue Américaine, Brussels. Victor Horta, architect.

44. Entrance to a large building, 127 rue de Longchamp. R. Gaillard,
architect.

45. A. Dondelinger. Entrances to a large building, 105 rue Jouffroy.
Théodore Petit, architect.

46. Entrance to a large building, 14 rue L'Abbé-de-l'Épée. G. Le Roy,
architect.

47. Entrance to "Castel Henriette." Hector Guimard, architect.

48. Carlton Hotel, 121 avenue des Champs-Élysées.

49. Entrance to a large building, 6 rue d'Athènes. Frederick Bertrand, architect.

50. Entrance to a town house, 190 boulevard Militaire, Ixelles-Brussels.
A. Méan, architect.

51. Entrance to a town house, 67 rue d'Espagne. Ernest Blérot, architect.

52. Entrance to a town house, 6 rue du Lac, Brussels. Ernest Delune,
architect.

53. Entrance to a town house, rue Vilan XIV. Ernest Blérot, architect.

54. Entrance to a town house, 188 boulevard Militaire, Ixelles-Brussels.
De Lestré de Fabribeckers, architect.

55. P. Desmedt. Entrance to a town house, 46 rue de Facqz. Paul Hankar,
architect.

56. Gate and fence of a private home, allée de la Robertsau, Strasbourg. Berninger & Krafft, architects.

57. Schwartz & Meurer. Greenhouse.

58. E. Robert. Entrance and fence of a town house, 197, bis, rue Saint-Charles. M. Porche, architect.

59. Entrance to the Royal Palace Hotel, 8 rue de Richelieu. Constant Lemaire, architect.

60. *Top:* A. Dondelinger. Entrance to a town house, 12 rue Sédillot.
J. Lavirotte, architect. *Bottom:* A. Dondelinger. Wrought-iron balcony of
an apartment house, 9 rue Claude-Chahu. Charles Klein, architect.

61. *Top:* Entrance and balcony of a town house. Victor Horta, architect.
Bottom: A. Dondelinger. Wrought-iron balcony of an apartment house, 9
rue Claude-Chahu. Charles Klein, architect.

62. E. Robert. Wrought-iron and copper grille panel.

63. E. Robert. Wrought-iron elevator gate (acquired by the Museum of
Decorative Arts in Copenhagen).

64. Entrance to an apartment house, 29 avenue Rapp. J. Lavirotte,
architect.

65. Entrance and balcony, Maison du Peuple, Brussels. Victor Horta, architect.

66. Entrance to a town house, avenue Jef-Lambeaux, Brussels.
G. Peereboom, architect.

67. Entrance to a town house, avenue Van Volxem, Forest. E. De Baus,
architect.

68. P. Desmedt. Entrance to a town house, 385 avenue Louise, Brussels.
Paul Hankar, architect.

69. Entrance to the Sulzer Frères Building, 7 avenue de la République.
Eugène Meyer, architect.

70. Schwartz & Meurer. Window of the Fiat building, 9 rue de la Paix.
E. Bertrand Père et Fils, architects.

71. J. Salvanhac. Entrance to an apartment house, 21 rue Monsieur.
Gustave Goy, architect.

72. J. Bogaerts. Wrought-iron door, balcony and basement window of a
town house, 21 avenue Louise, Brussels. P. Saintenoy, architect.

73. J. Salvanhac. Wrought-iron shop entrance and balconies, 14 rue d'Abbeville. E. Autant, architect.

74. Subway entrance, place de la Bastille. Hector Guimard, architect.

75. Entrance, 3 square Rapp. J. Lavirotte, architect.

76. Alfred Bellard. Elevator gate in the New York (Co.) Building. Morin
Goustiaux, architect.

77. Alfred Bellard. Entrance to the town house of Prince Roland Bonaparte,
avenue d'Iéna. E. & A. Janty, architects.

78. Alfred Bellard. Elevator gate in the New York (Co.) Building. Morin
Goustiaux, architect.

79. Elevator gate in a large building, 1 rue Mozart. Du Bois d'Auberville,
architect.

80. Lantern at the entrance of the Carlton Hotel, 121 avenue des Champs-Élysées.

81. Entrance to a large building, 12 rue Puvis-de-Chavannes. L. Roy,
architect.

82. Detail of the entrance of the Sulzer Frères Building, 7 avenue de la
République. Eugène Meyer, architect.

83. Detail of the stair railing of the Sulzer Frères Building, 7 avenue de la République. Eugène Meyer, architect.

84. E. Robert. Wrought-iron decorative panel and elevator gate.

85. Berlie. Cast-iron door of a mausoleum in the cemetery of Collonges-au-
Mont d'Or (Rhône). L. Rogniat, architect.

86. Helman. Entrance to an apartment house, boulevard du Nord.

87. Entrance to the Knopf building, Strasbourg. Berninger & Krafft,
architects.

88. E. Robert. Wrought-iron elevator gate.

89. Wrought-iron gate, 255 avenue de Longchamp. Ernest Blérot, architect.

90. Wrought-iron and gilt stair railings in a Brussels town house. Victor
Horta, architect.

91. Alfred Bellard. Stair in the library of Prince Roland Bonaparte.
Executed by "Maison Krieger," E. & A. Janty, architects.

92. Canopy support on the Sulzer Frères building, 7 avenue de la
République. Eugène Meyer, architect.

93. Detail of the entrance of a large building, 110 boulevard Raspail.
Eugène Chifflot, architect.

94. P. Desmedt. Wrought-iron aviary on an estate in Linkebeck. L. Govaerts, Brussels, architect.

95. P. Desmedt. Wrought-iron gate to a park, avenue de Tervueren,
Brussels. L. Govaerts, architect.

96. Entrance to a large building, 1 rue Mozart. Du Bois d'Auberville,
architect.

97. A. Dondelinger. Entrance to a large building, 132 rue de Courcelles.
Théodore Petit, architect.

98. Railings on the main stairway of a large building, 116 boulevard
Péreire. H. Tassu, architect.

99. Detail of a door handle, 110 boulevard Raspail. Eugène Chifflot, architect.

100. An apartment house in Broglie, France. Berninger & Krafft, architects.

101. P. Desmedt. The "Old England" department store, rue Montagne de la
Cour, Brussels. P. Saintenoy, architect, in collaboration with De Becker,
architect, and Wyhowski, engineer.

102. Wrought-iron balcony in a town house in Brussels. Victor Horta,
architect.

103. Entrance to a large building, 116 boulevard Péreire. H. Tassu, architect.

104. *Top:* A. Dondelinger. Wrought-iron stair railing, 29 avenue Rapp.
J. Lavirotte, architect. *Bottom:* E. Robert. Wrought-iron stair railing,
Vichy Theater. Charles Le Coeur, architect.

105. *Top:* A. Dondelinger. Wrought-iron stair railing, 29 avenue Rapp.
J. Lavirotte, architect. *Bottom:* E. Robert. Wrought-iron stair railing,
Vichy Theater. Charles Le Coeur, architect.

106. E. Robert. Details of panels from the entrance of the Vichy Theater.
Charles Le Coeur, architect.

107. D'Hière. Detail of a grille for a room.

108. *Top:* Gilon Frères. Stair railing in a town house; designed by Lalique.
L. & A. Feine, architects. *Bottom:* Wrought-iron stair railing in a town
house in Brussels. V. Horta, architect.

109. *Top:* Gilon Frères. Elevator cage in a town house, 40 Cours-la-Reine. Lalique, designer; L. & A. Feine, architects. *Bottom:* E. Robert. Wrought-iron stair railing. Charles Le Coeur, architect.

110. *Top:* Gilon Frères. Stair railing in a town house, 40 Cours-la-Reine.
Lalique, designer; L. & A. Feine, architects. *Bottom:* Schwartz & Meurer.
Lamp and railing.

111. *Top:* E. Robert. Detail of a wrought-iron panel with chasing. *Bottom:*
E. Robert. Detail of the railing for a funeral monument.

112. *Top:* Wrought-iron stair railing in a town house. V. Horta, architect.
Bottom: E. Robert. Wrought-iron communion railing in the Church of
Bougival. L. Magne, architect.

113. *Top:* E. Robert. Balcony. Xavier Schoellkopf, architect.
Bottom: E. Robert. Balustrade.

114. *Top and bottom:* Alfred Bellard. Details of balconies in the town house of Prince Roland Bonaparte, avenue d'Iéna.

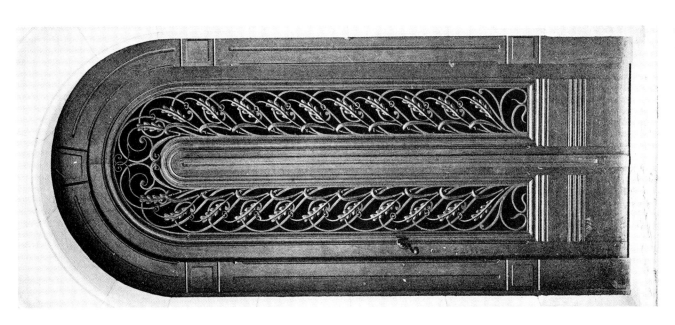

115. *Left:* E. Robert. Side entrance to the thermal springs at Vichy. Charles Le Coeur, architect.
Center: Schwartz & Meurer. Lamp. *Right:* Side entrance to the thermal springs at Vichy.
Charles Le Coeur, architect.

116. *Top:* E. Robert. Stair railing at the thermal springs at Vichy. Charles Le Coeur, architect.
Bottom: Wrought-iron stair railing with chasing. L. Majorelle, architect.

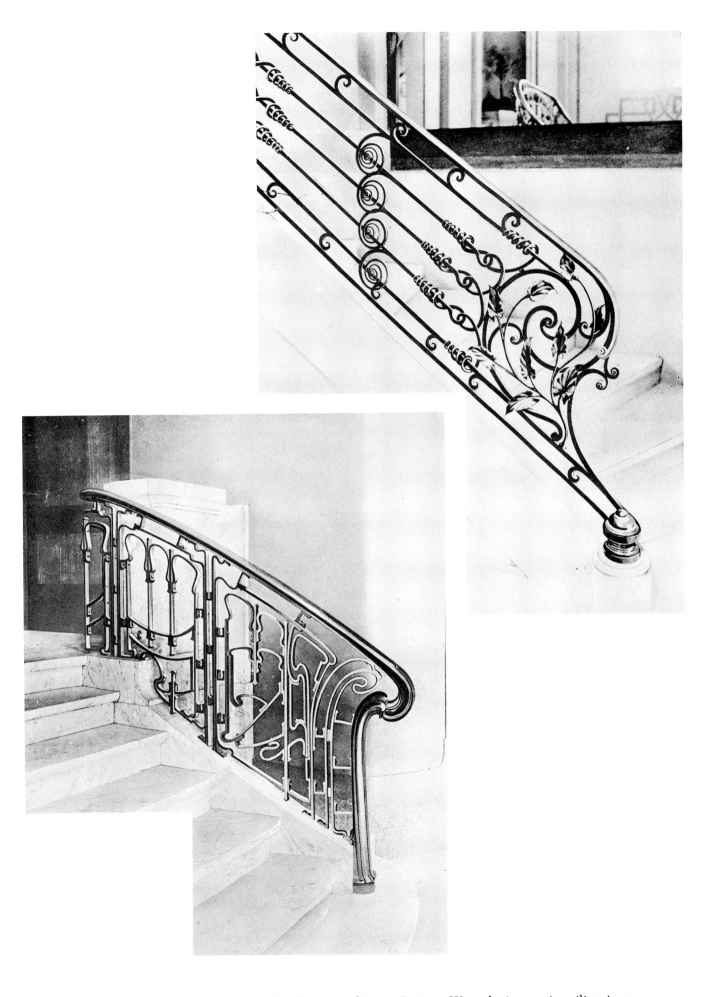

117. *Top:* Stair railing. Charles Le Coeur, architect. *Bottom:* Wrought-iron stair railing in a town house, 520 avenue Louise. Victor Horta, architect.

118. E. Robert. Wrought-iron elevator gate in a town house, 38 rue Condorcet. A. Fiquet, architect.

119. E. Robert. Wrought-iron stand.